JAKE DELHOMME, STEPHEN DAVIS, BRAD HOOVER, STEVE SMITH, MUHSIN MUHAMMAD, WESLEY WALLS, JORDAN GROSS, BLAKE BROCKERMEYER, MIKE WAHLE, KEVIN DONNALLEY, RYAN KALIL, JULIUS PEPPERS, MIKE RUCKER, KRIS JENKINS, BRENTSON BUCKNER, KEVIN GREENE, SAM MILLS, JON BEASON, CHRIS GAMBLE, ERIC DAVIS, MIKE MINTER, DEON GRANT, JOHN KASAY, TODD SAUERBRUN, JAKE DELHOMME, STEPHEN DAVIS, BRAD HOOVER, STEVE SMITH, MUHSIN MUHAMMAD, WESLEY WALLS, JORDAN

THE STORY OF THE CAROLINA PANTHERS

THE STORY OF THE CAROLINA PANTHERS

BY JIM WHITING

CREATIVE EDUCATION / CREATIVE PAPERBACKS

PUBLISHED BY CREATIVE EDUCATION AND CREATIVE PAPERBACKS
P.O. BOX 227, MANKATO, MINNESOTA 56002
CREATIVE EDUCATION AND CREATIVE PAPERBACKS ARE IMPRINTS OF THE
CREATIVE COMPANY
WWW.THECREATIVECOMPANY.US

DESIGN AND PRODUCTION BY BLUE DESIGN (WWW.BLUEDES.COM)
ART DIRECTION BY RITA MARSHALL
PRINTED IN CHINA

PHOTOGRAPHS BY AP IMAGES (ASSOCIATED PRESS), GETTY IMAGES (BRIAN
BAHR, AL BELLO/ALLSPORT, DOUG BENC, REX BROWN, BRETT
CARLSEN/STRINGER, LARRY FRENCH, GRANT HALVERSON, JEFF HAYNES/AFP,
JED JACOBSOHN, CRAIG JONES, STEVEN KING/ICON SPORTSWIRE, STREETER
LECKA, BRAD MANGIN/SI, RONALD MARTINEZ, REINHOLD MATAY, RONALD C.
MODRA/SPORTS IMAGERY, PATRICK MURPHY-RACEY/SI, CHRISTIAN PETERSEN,
JEFF SINER/CHARLOTTE OBSERVER/MCT, PAUL SPINELLI, MATTHEW
STOCKMAN, DILIP VISHWANAT, MICHAEL ZAGARIS/SAN FRANCISCO 49ERS)

NAMES: WHITING, JIM, AUTHOR.
TITLE: THE STORY OF THE CAROLINA PANTHERS / JIM WHITING.
SERIES: NFL TODAY.
INCLUDES INDEX.
SUMMARY: THIS HIGH-INTEREST HISTORY OF THE NATIONAL FOOTBALL
LEAGUE'S CAROLINA PANTHERS HIGHLIGHTS MEMORABLE GAMES, SUMMARIZES
SEASONAL TRIUMPHS AND DEFEATS, AND FEATURES STANDOUT PLAYERS SUCH
AS CAM NEWTON.
IDENTIFIERS: LCCN 2018059125 / ISBN 978-1-64026-134-1 (HARDCOVER) / ISBN
978-1-62832-697-0 (PBK) / ISBN 978-1-64000-252-4 (EBOOK)
SUBJECTS: LCSH: CAROLINA PANTHERS (FOOTBALL TEAM)—HISTORY—
JUVENILE LITERATURE.
CLASSIFICATION: LCC GV956.C27 W47 2019 / DDC 796.332/640975676—DC23

FIRST EDITION HC 9 8 7 6 5 4 3 2 1
FIRST EDITION PBK 9 8 7 6 5 4 3 2 1

COVER: CAM NEWTON
PAGE 2: CHRISTIAN MCCAFFREY
PAGES 6-7: DESHAUN FOSTER

TABLE OF CONTENTS

GRIDIRON GREATS

DEFENSE AT ITS BEST

The Carolina Panthers impressed football experts in 1996. The Panthers were an expansion team in the National Football League (NFL). It was just their second year. New teams in any pro sport normally need several years to develop. But the Panthers won five of their first nine games that year. Amazingly, they also won their next six games. They knocked off the San Francisco 49ers during the streak. This was important. Going into the final regular-season game, Carolina and San Francisco were tied atop the National Football Conference (NFC) Western Division. The division champion would have a first-round bye in the play-offs. That team would also host the second round. The Panthers had beaten the 49ers twice during the season. This meant that if both teams won their final games, Carolina owned the tiebreaker.

But Carolina faced a formidable foe. The Pittsburgh Steelers were the defending American Football Conference (AFC) champions. The Panthers scored first. Quarterback Kerry Collins threw a nine-yard touchdown pass to tight end Wesley Walls. Carolina added two more points on a safety. But Pittsburgh struck back. It scored two touchdowns in the second quarter. Carolina followed halftime with three drives. Each one ended with a short field goal by John Kasay. These gave the Panthers an 18–14 lead. Then it was the Steelers' turn. They drove to the Panthers' six-yard line. Less than a minute remained.

All season, the Panthers had relied on their smothering defense. It was designed by head coach Dom Capers. They rarely gave up more than 20 points in a game. Could they keep the Steelers out of the end zone? Carolina defenders stuffed two Pittsburgh running plays. On third down, Steelers quarterback Kordell Stewart spotted a receiver

LEFT: LINEBACKER SAM MILLS

GRIDIRON GREATS ᵛ
STEVE'S SPRINT

Quarterback Steve Beuerlein was not known for his running ability. Yet a famous Beuerlein run is fondly remembered as "The Draw." The play occurred in December 1999. The Panthers were playing the Green Bay Packers. Only five seconds were left. The Panthers trailed by four. They had the ball on the five-yard line. Coach George Seifert called a quarterback draw. "They'll never expect it," he said. Beuerlein announced the play in the huddle. His teammates were shocked. He dropped back as if to pass. Then he followed his blockers into the end zone. Carolina won the game.

CAROLINA PANTHERS

11

PAT TERRELL AND SAM MILLS

"HERE'S A TEAM THAT WASN'T EVEN A TEAM THREE YEARS AGO, AND NOW THEY ARE JUST ONE GAME AWAY FROM THE SUPER BOWL."

—SPORTSCASTER JOHN MADDEN

in the end zone. His pass was on target. But Panthers defensive back Chad Cota jumped in front of the receiver. He intercepted the ball. Carolina's victory was sealed. "[That play] was a fitting ending," Capers told reporters. "It showed the strength and the will of our guys."

The victory gave the Panthers an extra week to rest and prepare. They faced the Dallas Cowboys in the divisional round. Late in the game, Carolina held a six-point lead. The Cowboys drove toward the end zone. Once again, the defense saved the day. Safety Pat Terrell picked off a Dallas pass. Kasay kicked his fourth field goal. The Panthers won! Few people could have foreseen such sudden success by a new team. "Here's a team that wasn't even a team three years ago," said sportscaster John Madden, "and now they are just one game away from the Super Bowl."

GRIDIRON GREATS ∨
WHEN SIZE DOESN'T MATTER

The NFL's top receivers tend to be big men. This helps them shield defenders on short passes. They are also fast and agile. Receivers need to jump higher than everyone on deep throws. Steve Smith was an undersized receiver. But his agility and competitive nature made up for his stature. He was not afraid to catch passes in traffic. His fancy footwork allowed him to break away from coverage. "You get your full money's worth with a guy like that," said New York Giants defensive back Brent Alexander. "He blocks, he catches the ball, he runs with the ball—he does everything."

81

81 CAREER RECEIVING TOUCHDOWNS

219

219 GAMES PLAYED

15

SAM MILLS

TWO STATES, ONE TEAM

n 1663, King Charles II of England gave some of his supporters land in America. They named the colony Carolina in his honor. (Carolina is a form of the Latin name for Charles.) Eventually, the colony split into two states. In 1993, North and South Carolina had a reason to join together. The NFL awarded an expansion franchise to Jerry Richardson. He had played in the NFL. He was raised in North Carolina. But he had gone to college in South Carolina. The franchise would be located in

266

266 GAMES PLAYED AS OF 2018

159.5

159.5 CAREER SACKS AS OF 2018

JULIUS PEPPERS
DEFENSIVE END

PANTHERS SEASONS:
2002–09, 2017–18
HEIGHT: 6-FOOT-7
WEIGHT: 295 POUNDS

GRIDIRON GREATS v
SPICING THINGS UP

Julius Peppers played basketball for the University of North Carolina. The skills he developed on the hardwood helped him on the gridiron. Peppers sprinted around blockers. He used quick moves to sneak through them. Sometimes, he just ran over them as he notched quarterback sacks. He was also willing to drive running backs into the ground. He used his height, long arms, and leaping ability to his advantage. He could bat down passes and block field goal tries. Explaining his style, Peppers said, "You've got to be disciplined. You have to be under control going in there but be aggressive at the same time."

CAROLINA PANTHERS

KERRY COLLINS

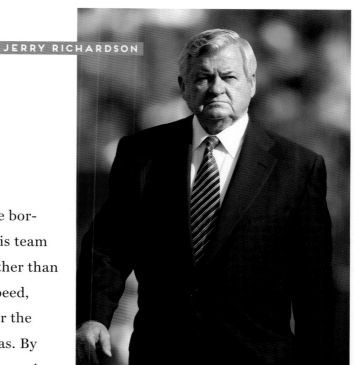

Charlotte, North Carolina. This city sits near the border of the two states. Richardson chose to call his team Carolina. This represented the entire region, rather than a single state. He wanted a mascot known for speed, power, and cunning. He chose Panthers to honor the big cats that were once abundant in the Carolinas. By coincidence, the other expansion team that year was in Jacksonville, Florida. That team also selected a big-cat name: Jaguars.

Carolina picked its team from a list of other NFL teams' players in an expansion draft. Cornerbacks Rod Smith and Tim McKyer joined Carolina. Wide receiver Mark Carrier and nose tackle Greg Kragen also became Panthers. In the 1995 NFL Draft, Carolina selected Kerry Collins. The quarterback had led Penn State to an undefeated season. Few people were surprised when Carolina lost its first five games. But the Panthers pounced on 7 of their next 11 opponents. They finished the season 7–9. It was the best-ever record for a first-year NFL team.

The next season opened at Charlotte's new Ericsson Stadium. Six massive bronze panthers guarded the

"FROM THE TIME YOU WALK INTO THIS PLACE, YOU FEEL INVINCIBLE. THE 'FANS WON'T LET US LOSE."

—LINEBACKER KEVIN GREENE

entrances. "I love the big cats," said tackle Blake Brockermeyer. "They make the place look mean." Opponents soon learned just how mean the Panthers could be. "From the time you walk into this place, you feel invincible," said linebacker Kevin Greene. "The fans won't let us lose." The Panthers won all eight regular season home games. They won the playoff game against Dallas, too. But the NFC Championship Game brought them to Green Bay. They faced the Packers in sub-zero temperatures. Carolina's offense went cold. Its Super Bowl dreams ended with a 30–13 defeat. "This was one time when home-field advantage really counted," said Jerry Richardson.

FOX LEADS
THE CATS

DEFENSIVE END SEAN GILBERT

Fans expected more success the following season. But the Panthers slipped to 7–9 in 1997. They fell to 4–12 in 1998. Injuries and disputes destroyed the team's winning chemistry. The Panthers started 1999 at 2–5. After that, the team changed to "West Coast Offense." It focused more on passing the ball than rushing. Quarterback Steve Beuerlein threw short passes all around the field. He completed 343 of 571 tosses. He piled up 4,436 yards and 36 touchdowns. The new strategy changed the course of the season. The Panthers finished with an 8–8 record. They barely missed the playoffs. "It was a great run for us," said

JAKE DELHOMME
QUARTERBACK

PANTHERS SEASONS: 2003-09
HEIGHT: 6-FOOT-2
WEIGHT: 215 POUNDS

GRIDIRON GREATS v
FOURTH-QUARTER
CONFIDENCE

Jake Delhomme's overall statistics usually ranked him as an average NFL quarterback. But in the fourth quarter, Delhomme was truly special. "You have to believe that you have the ability [to perform in the clutch] because, if not, this league will eat you up," Delhomme said. "You have to have confidence to know that you have done this already a few times, and you can do it again." Delhomme showed his confidence in the Panthers' drive to the Super Bowl in 2003. He led them to victory on the final possession eight times.

103

126

126 CAREER PASSING TOUCHDOWNS

27

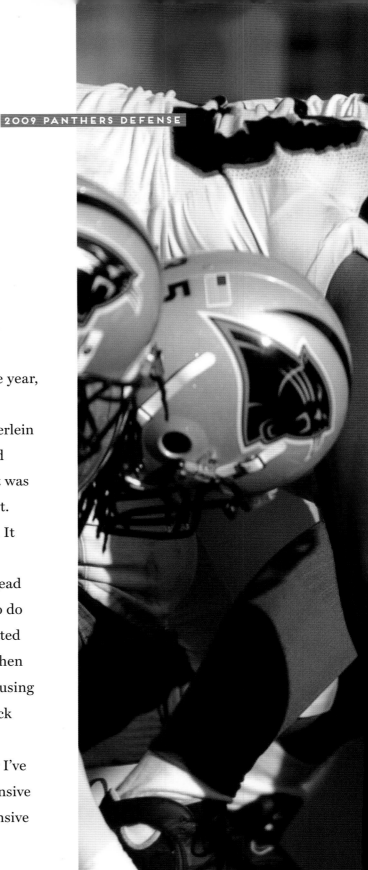

Beuerlein. "A lot of people wrote us off early in the year, but our guys kept scrapping."

The Panthers finished the 2000 season 7–9. Beuerlein left after that. Rookie quarterback Chris Weinke led Carolina to an opening-week victory in 2001. But it was the team's only win of the season. Carolina fell apart. It suffered late-game collapses and overtime losses. It finished 1–15.

Carolina hired defensive specialist John Fox as head coach. Fox told his players that he expected them to do two things: work hard and have fun. Then he repeated one of his favorite quotes: "This game is only fun when you win." Fox aimed to build a winning team by focusing on defense. The Panthers had the second overall pick in the 2002 Draft. They chose defensive end Julius Peppers. "Peppers is probably the most athletic guy I've played with since I've been in the league," said defensive tackle Brentson Buckner. "You have a guy in a defensive

STEVE SMITH

lineman's body who has feet like a defensive back and the speed of a safety." On offense, Carolina followed veteran quarterback Rodney Peete. Experienced wide receivers Muhsin Muhammad and Steve Smith gave the team a boost. It won its first three games. Then it suffered a series of injuries. The team lost its next eight matches. It finished 7–9.

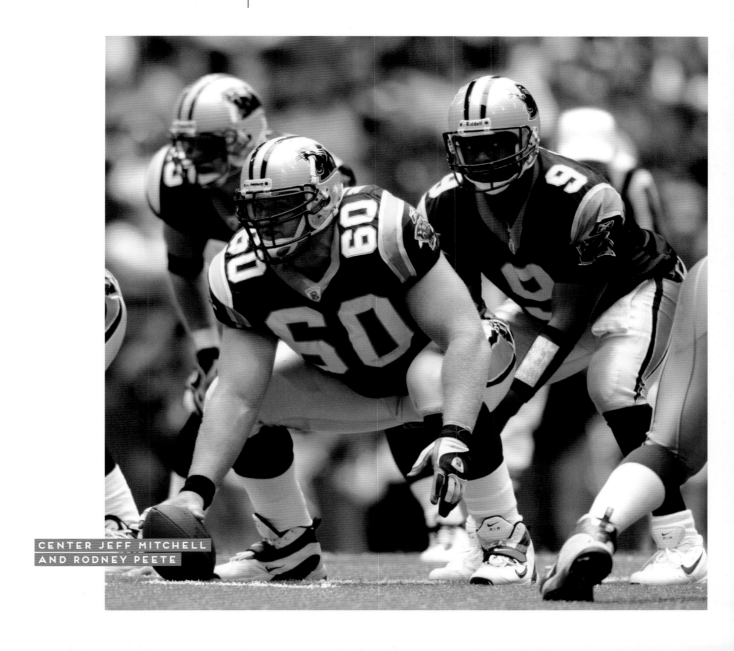

CENTER JEFF MITCHELL
AND RODNEY PEETE

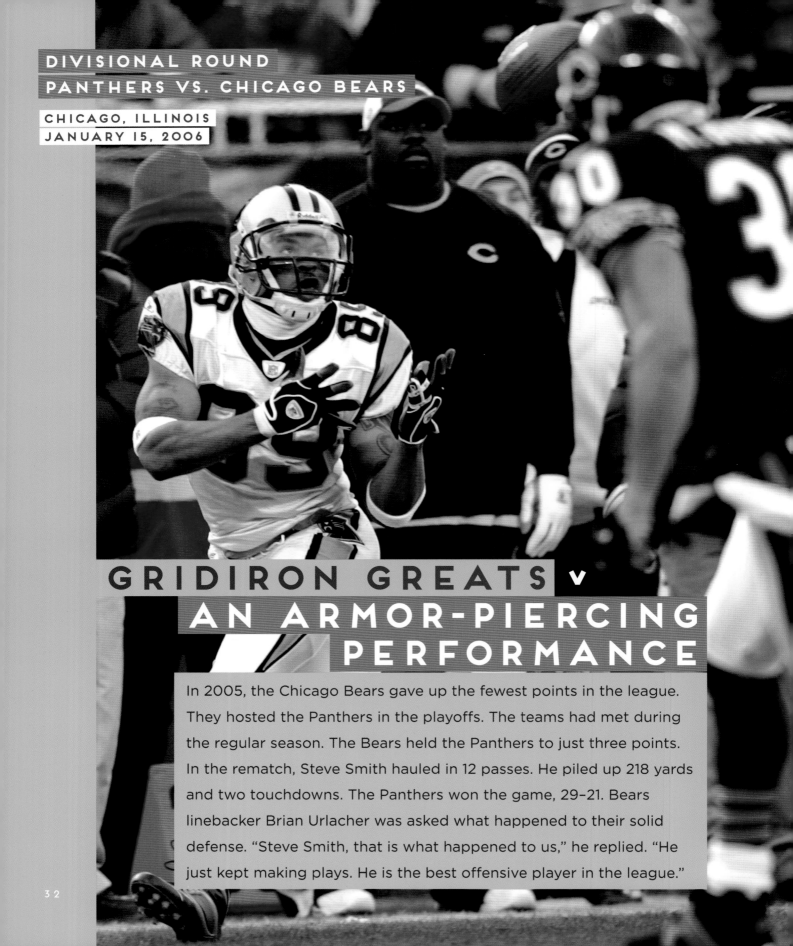

GRIDIRON GREATS ᵛ
AN ARMOR-PIERCING PERFORMANCE

In 2005, the Chicago Bears gave up the fewest points in the league. They hosted the Panthers in the playoffs. The teams had met during the regular season. The Bears held the Panthers to just three points. In the rematch, Steve Smith hauled in 12 passes. He piled up 218 yards and two touchdowns. The Panthers won the game, 29–21. Bears linebacker Brian Urlacher was asked what happened to their solid defense. "Steve Smith, that is what happened to us," he replied. "He just kept making plays. He is the best offensive player in the league."

12

12 PASSES CAUGHT VS. BEARS 1/15/06

244

244 TOTAL YARDS VS. BEARS 1/15/06

Before the 2003 season,
Carolina signed powerful running back Stephen Davis.
It also added sure-handed wide receiver Ricky Proehl.
Quarterback Jake Delhomme joined the Panthers, too.
Fox knew he would be taking a chance on Delhomme.
He had seen little playing time as a backup with the New
Orleans Saints. But Fox was impressed with Delhomme's
poise. The quarterback had the ability to throw long
passes. That opened up the offense and kept opposing
defenders off balance.

SUPER BOWL BOUND

The Panthers began 2003 with two heart-stopping victories. Local sportswriters dubbed them the "Cardiac Cats." The rest of the season was just as exciting. Carolina earned two overtime victories. It rallied for last-minute wins twice. The team won 11 games. The Panthers also earned the NFC South Division title. They raced into the playoffs. First, they dispatched the Cowboys, 29–10. Then they butted heads with the St. Louis Rams. The close contest went into double-overtime. Delhomme sealed the win with a touchdown pass to Smith.

The following week, the Panthers faced the Philadelphia Eagles. It was the NFC Championship. Buckner exhorted his teammates: "Everyone says we're not supposed to win. I want us to take the whole city [of Philadelphia] and shut it down!" They did. It was a defensive struggle. Carolina won, 14–3. It earned a spot in Super Bowl XXXVIII. The Panthers would play the New England Patriots.

DEANGELO WILLIAMS

That Super Bowl was one of the most exciting ever. The lead bounced back and forth. Delhomme hit Proehl with a 12-yard pass to tie the score at 29. Just over a minute remained. But it was enough time for New England to drive the ball into scoring range. The Patriots kicked the game-winning field goal.

The next season, the Panthers were set on improving their Super Bowl performance. But their hopes burst during the first game. Both Davis and Smith suffered season-ending injuries. The Panthers lost seven of their first eight games. They rebounded to a 7–9 record. But they missed the playoffs.

The Panthers roared back to the playoffs in 2005. They won 11 games. In the Wild Card round, the Carolina defense completely stopped the favored New York Giants. The Panthers shut them out, 23–0. A victory over the Chicago Bears put the Panthers back in the NFC title game. But their run of success came to an abrupt end. The Seattle Seahawks crushed Carolina, 34–14. "I don't know if we ran out of gas," said Fox. "I'm not sure what the problem was. Their defense played tremendous. They stopped us cold."

That disappointment seemed to spill into 2006. Carolina finished 8–8. It was one victory away from the playoffs. Matters got worse in 2007. Delhomme went down with a season-ending elbow injury. The Panthers finished 7–9. In 2008, though, the Cats were back. Delhomme was healthy. Supporting him were running backs Jonathan Stewart and DeAngelo Williams. They were nicknamed "Smash and Dash." Together, they formed a dynamic one-two rushing punch. The Panthers streaked to a 12–4 record. They earned a first-round bye in the playoffs. But they came out flat in the divisional round. They hosted the Arizona Cardinals. Delhomme threw five interceptions. The Panthers lost, 33–13. Delhomme's interception problems continued into 2009. He left town after the 8–8 season. The next season was nearly the worst in team history. The team burned through four quarterbacks. When the smoke cleared, Carolina was left with a 2–14 record.

JONATHAN STEWART

CAM COMES ON BOARD

That bad season had an upside. Carolina received the first overall pick in the 2011 Draft. They selected enormous quarterback Cam Newton. At 6-foot-5 and 245 pounds, he was built like a defensive end. Plus, he was remarkably athletic. Skeptics questioned how he would adjust to the NFL. The rookie came out firing. He was helped by Smith and sure-handed tight end Greg Olsen. Newton threw for 4,051 yards. But the Panthers won just 2 of their first 10 games. On the bright side, four losses were by a touchdown or less. The Panthers were out of the playoffs. But

CAROLINA PANTHERS

GRIDIRON GREATS v
A NEW MIDDLE NAME?

Cam Newton's middle name is Jerrell. Based on his accomplishments, it could easily be "Only." In college, he won the Heisman Trophy and a national championship. The same year, he was the first overall pick in the NFL Draft. In a 2015 game, he passed for 340 yards and five touchdowns. In the same game, he racked up 100 rushing yards. That season, he passed for 35 touchdowns and rushed for 10 more. Newton is the only NFL quarterback to have done these things. And let's not even get started on "First." At least 20 statements could begin "Cam Newton is the first … "

CAM NEWTON
QUARTERBACK

PANTHERS SEASONS: 2011-PRESENT
HEIGHT: 6-FOOT-5
WEIGHT: 245

CAROLINA PANTHERS

43

they gained confidence by winning four of their last six games. "It's unfortunate that we're playing like this at the end when we let a lot of games slip away," said tackle Jordan Gross. "[But] it's exciting for the future. I love the look of this team right now."

In 2012, the team added linebacker Luke Kuechly. He became the Defensive Rookie of the Year. Still, Carolina managed only seven wins for the season. A 1–3 start in 2013 suggested more of the same. But the Panthers surged to win 11 of the 12 remaining games. The season ended on a sour note, though. The 49ers ousted them from the playoffs. The team fell to 7–8–1 in 2014. However, the rest of the NFC South performed even worse. Remarkably, the Panthers were in the playoffs. As division champions, they hosted Arizona in the Wild Card. They won, 27–16. But the Seahawks knocked them out in the next round.

Everything clicked in 2015. Newton was named the league's Most Valuable Player (MVP). He led Carolina to a 15–1 mark. The NFL had gone to a 16-game schedule in 1978. Only 6 other teams had won 15 games since then. Carolina flew through the playoffs. The Panthers were headed to Super Bowl 50! They faced off against the Denver Broncos. They were favored to win. But Newton was sacked six times. The team had four turnovers. Carolina lost, 24–10. The next year, the team struggled with injuries. The Panthers finished just 6–10. They clawed their way to 11–5 in 2017. But the Saints booted

LEFT: LINEBACKER JAMES ANDERSON

LUKE KUECHLY

WIDE RECEIVER D. J. MOORE

them out of the playoffs. In 2018, running back Christian McCaffrey emerged as a solid rusher. But as a team, the Panthers dropped to a 7–9 finish.

The Carolina Panthers' relatively short history is filled with remarkable success. Tough players such as Jake Delhomme, Steve Smith, and Luke Kuechly have always pushed the team to succeed. From an NFC Championship Game appearance in its second year to the near defeat of the Patriots in Super Bowl XXXVIII, Carolina has proven it isn't intimidated by big moments or powerhouse opponents. As the Panthers continue fielding fiery gridiron combatants, fans in both North and South Carolina will have plenty to roar about.

NFC CHAMPIONSHIPS

2003, 2015

CAROLINA PANTHERS

https://www.panthers.com/

NFL: CAROLINA PANTHERS TEAM PAGE

http://www.nfl.com/teams/carolinapanthers/profile?team=CAR

CAROLINA PANTHERS

INDEX

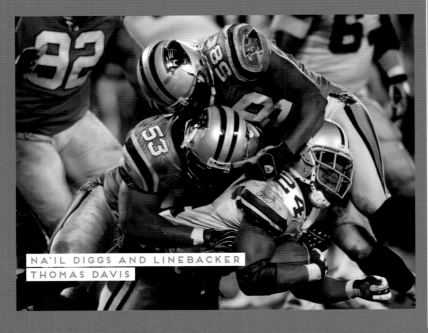

NA'IL DIGGS AND LINEBACKER THOMAS DAVIS